What the Gargoyle Sees

What the Gargoyle Sees

Poems by

Gene Twaronite

© 2021 Gene Twaronite. All rights reserved. This material may not be reproduced in any form, published, reprinted, recorded, performed, broadcast, rewritten or redistributed without the explicit permission of Gene Twaronite. All such actions are strictly prohibited by law.

Cover design by Shay Culligan

ISBN: 978-1-952326-86-8

Kelsay Books
502 South 1040 East, A-119
American Fork, Utah, 84003

Acknowledgments

The author gratefully acknowledges the editors of the following print and online journals, where these poems first appeared:

Eternal Haunted Summer: "Four O'clock Light"

Ginosko Literary Journal: "What the Gargoyle Sees"

James Gunn's Ad Astra: "Journey to the Center of the Poem"

New Myths: "The Persistence of Pheromones," "The Yellow Snake," "Trash Picker on Mars," "Wizards at Heart"

Not One of Us: "Free Universe"

Star 82 Review: "An Eye-Pleasing Assemblage"

Starline: "A Little Planet of My Own," "Afterlife,"

The Museum of Unwearable Shoes (Kelsay Books): "Where Words Go to Die"

Typehouse Literary Magazine: "The Headless Tin Soldier"

Wilderness House Literary Review: "Galaxy Flight to Midnight," "The Last Fact"

Contents

Wizards at Heart	11
Trash Picker on Mars	13
Prayer to Cthulhu	15
The Headless Tin Soldier	16
Journey to the Center of the Poem	18
From Your Mouth a Flower Will Come	20
What the Gargoyle Sees	21
The Last Fact	22
Azathoth	24
Extinction Sale	25
The Yellow Snake	26
Four O'clock Light	27
Loki's Lament	28
Catching the Venom	29
Free Universe	30
A Little Planet of My Own	31
Galaxy Flight to Midnight	32
The Case of the Missing Pea	33
The Persistence of Pheromones	35
Where Words Go to Die	38
Ways to Kill Time	40
An Eye-Pleasing Assemblage	42
Afterlife	43

Wizards at Heart

A flash of light bursts
from the wizard's wand,
ancient powers unleashed—
a legerdemain of photons
enchanting us in the darkness
of our deepest longings.

We know the magic is not real
yet we believe it still.

We are all magicians at heart,
conjuring up gods and worlds—
even our own existence—
out of the power of mind.

We are each a wholly trinity
of word, thought, and image
endlessly inventing our lives
with new realities.

We hurl ourselves into space,
bending its fabric to fit
the models we construct.
We are tricksters of time
stretching moments to infinity.
Dinosaurs dance on Broadway
while zombies never die.

We foresee our future in heaven
while hosts of our enemies
descend by decree into hells
filled with delicious horrors.

Modern day magi, we come
bearing gifts for the child within.
We cast our spells against the sun
and tides, commanding them to stop.
And who shall say they won't
when you're a wizard?

Trash Picker on Mars

In the dim time before dawn
the woman clamped her metal
fingers over a beer bottle.
Her buckets overflowing with
litter from a dying world,
she sat and stared at
the alien landscape of asphalt.
The stars had all faded
except for the one red light
of Mars still defying the sun.
The woman smiled at
the mythical planet now
defrocked of its canals
and green men by Carl Sagan
and the Legion of Reason.
But still she dreamed.
In her electric cart she glided
over the red-gold deserts
of ancient Barsoom,
past the fairy towers
of Grand Canal and the
monoliths of Helium where
a once great race of Martians
lived, played, and died,
filling the canyons of
Valles Marineris with
the excess of their empty lives.
Out of habit she picked up
a fluted green shard, then
laughed and flung it along
with her buckets into
the trash heap of lost Martians.

Through the dark grottoes of
Great Rift Valley she roved to
the shores of Mare Sirenum,
whose salty crust reminded her
of past ruins and distant times
when she could still cry.
For a moment she stared at
the sun, weak and small as it
rose above Olympus Mons,
igniting her in a ruddy glow.
She was the Princess of Mars
and there were still a few
unhatched eggs inside her.
And at the edge of
Candor Chasm she
bared her heart to
the silent, scouring winds.
Then into the dawn
she drove to begin
her new race of Martians.

Prayer to Cthulhu

Oh, great Cthulhu, with tentacled face, we
beseech you to save the blue earth from
this noxious race of arrogant apes
who care not a whit if the rest of life
exists at all, forever taking,
not giving, breeding like cockroaches,
defiling everything they touch, filling
the air with their carbon breath
as forests burn and seas rise.

Too long has this pimple of
humanity festered—time
to end the Anthropocene Age.

Awaken from your dreams and take your place.
The stars are all aligned. Time to turn
the page and begin your master race.

We cultists stand ready to engage. Time
to rise from the sea and vent your rage.

The Headless Tin Soldier

Revisiting Hans Christian Andersen

Is this what it means to be steadfast,
silently shouldering your tiny gun
with unshakable tinny hands
through the long dark tunnel
and the fish's cold stomach,
never showing fear or tears
or any sign to prove you're
not just a lump of lead?

Might as well be headless instead of
one-legged for all it matters.

You wouldn't even shout to save yourself—
too improper for a man in uniform.
Easier to blame it on the
little black goblin in the snuffbox.
Blame him as well for the little boy
who threw you into the fire.

What are you waiting for?
Tell your little dancer you love her
before it's too late, before that draft
blows her into the fire next to you
and you burn together in
that horrible heat where flame
meets feelings never expressed,
just so the maid could find you there—
a little tin heart
and your dancer's spangle
burned as black as coal.

If I were that boy,
I would have thrown
you into the fire myself.

Journey to the Center of the Poem

To Jules Verne

Dare I follow the cryptic runes of Saknussemm,
descending into the shadow-kissed crater
seeking unknown tunnels to the center?

Why undertake a journey
so inconvenient or improbable?

One does not need to climb
a volcano in Iceland to find
pathways worthy of exploration.

Indeed, why journey at all
and not let Life come to us
in prepackaged servings?

And what's so great about a point
equidistant from the ends?
Surely there are plenty of things
to be found in the prelude—
those first few tentative steps in the darkness
when the enormity of your task
fills the heart with dread and you
wish you'd never left home.

But, tired and thirsty, you plug on
through the arid lonely tunnels
until realizing you're hopelessly lost.

And let us not forget the finale.
Isn't getting there what really counts?
Just tell me how it ends.

Did they meet their fate bravely?
Did they finally escape?
Did the love birds get married?
And was there some purpose to it all?

But the poem knows otherwise.
Only in the center will you find
subterranean caverns bathed in strange light,
vast oceans teeming with sea monsters,
forests filled with petrified trees, mastodons,
man-apes, and other creatures from your past.

There you must come to terms
with whatever perils lie in wait
around the next bend.

No one can save you from yourself.
It will all end here, lost and forgotten
in the bowels of an unexplored world,
or you'll take the journey to its conclusion,
your raft swept by the rushing waters
into the volcano's chimney,
carried on a rising surge of magma
by the primal heat of creation—
up, up, up until ejected in elation
into the clear blue sky above Stromboli.

From Your Mouth a Flower Will Come

The gift that I give you is this: at every word you speak, from your mouth a flower will come, or else a precious stone.
—Charles Perrault, "The Fairies," The Complete Fairy Tales

It might not always be
a rose or a diamond
for some words merit
only roadside wildflowers
or storm-tossed sea glass
and contrary to the moral
a gentle word is
seldom strong enough
to move a heart
made of stone
but at least you
don't have to worry that
at every word you speak
a toad or a viper will come.

What the Gargoyle Sees

You think it easy
leering down all day
with bestial gape
on the war below
as a widow cries
for a third son lost,
a one-eyed child
with half a face
stares up and smiles
at me before he dies.

The Last Fact

You might think it
one of those folks
like earth is round
or the sky is blue,
but those two died
years ago
in a rest home
where old facts go
to die in peace.
Everyone knows
earth is flat
and the sky any
color you want.
Like his parents—
death and old age—
he was stubborn
till the end,
hiding out in
dark taverns
of falsehood
and innuendo
drinking absinthe
to forget, but
forget he could not,
no more than
a forge can forget
what it fires,
or a sieve forget
what it filters.
Reality police
caught up one day
and brought him in
for questioning.
They beat the truth

out of him till
there was nothing left
but skin and bones
and a shiny red stain,
as the sun sank
in the east
and the stars shone
from the heavens
like distant campfires.

Azathoth

that amorphous blight of nethermost confusion which blasphemes and bubbles at the center of all infinity...amidst the muffled, maddening beating of vile drums...
—H.P. Lovecraft, *The Dream-Quest of Unknown Kadath*

Some say it exists at the center of our galaxy
in hidden realms of black infinity.
But it's far closer than you think,
existing in the thin layer between
the presumed regularity of
all that you hold dear
and the random demonic
particles that bubble in
and out of existence
to the mad beat of drums.

Extinction Sale

Stylishly silly two-clawed Tyrannosaurus arms
Irish elk antlers in matching intertwined sets
Great auk down so light and fluffy it disappears
Rhino horns freshly ground to cure everything
Oversized brains barely used since replaced with AI

The Yellow Snake

I can take you further than a ship.
—Antoine de Saint-Exupéry, *The Little Prince*

I liked him from the start.
People don't stop and talk
with snakes anymore, especially
about things that matter.

He wished to go home to
his little planet and the vain
silly rose he loved
more than life itself.

He asked me about my poison
and thought I was his savior.
But I wanted only to tell him a story
to live in for a time and forget.

He tried to make me bite,
but I slipped past him in a yellow flash.
I saw him faint and fall to the sand.
But he did not die.

He thought his body was
too heavy and his planet too far.
He thought he needed poison
to leave behind his mortal shell.

But he had everything he needed,
right there inside him.
As he made his little planet live for me,
so he made it live again for himself.

And you don't need a snake for that.

Four O'clock Light

In the four o'clock light of a fall afternoon
The realm of reason gives way to wonder.
The vision of old is gone too soon.

Stone lichens read like an ancient rune
Of Odin casting my thoughts asunder
In the four o'clock light of a fall afternoon.

Do I dare emerge from my sane cocoon
To mine the ruins of a mythic world under
In the four o'clock light of a fall afternoon?

Is it Loki who tricks my spirit to swoon
And feeds this phantasmagoric hunger?
The vision of old is gone too soon.

I wish to ride in Mani's chariot moon
And wield the mighty hammer of thunder.
The vision of old is gone too soon.

For an instant the solid rock is hewn
As the inner child is freed to wander
In the four o'clock light of a fall afternoon.
The vision of old is gone too soon.

Loki's Lament

Loathed and unloved, I am forsaken,
a god unworthy of adoration.
And what was my terrible crime?
Was it that I fathered the great serpent
Jormungand, Thor's eternal curse?
Was it my role in Balder's death,
when I only wished to scare him?
Yes, it was I who brought the giants
and betrayed the gods at Ragnarok,
but they deserved it.

No, it was something far worse.
Inseminated by the stallion Svadilfari,
I mothered Sleipnir,
Odin's beloved eight-legged horse.
And I once ate the heart of a woman
so evil I could not help myself,
and because of this I gave birth
to every female monster who's ever lived.

But that I should give birth
violated all the rule books
of god and man, and that
they would never forgive.

Catching the Venom

Oh, good Sigyn, no matter how long you hold
the bowl, there will always be more venom,
doomed to fall drop by drop on poor Loki's face.
Once more, you leave the cave to empty it
as your husband writhes in pain at your absence.
Dutifully you play your part, again and again,
until the end of days or at least until you
finally realize he's not the husband you thought
and leave the cave for good as he shouts in virulent rage
for you to return, but you don't.

Free Universe

It was a nice space
as universes go—
everything was free there,
from love, will, and time
to lunch, radicals, and verse.
But the cost was too dear,
it could not last,
as even the strong force
was freed of its role
and things flew apart.
They had a big sale
but no one came,
so they closed their doors
and blinked goodnight.

A Little Planet of My Own

My planet is a trifle bigger than
the one the Little Prince lives on.
Instead of just three, it has
a dozen volcanoes which erupt
in iridescent salute every time I
visit and never need cleaning.
Mine has a waterfall that falls
straight up into the sky where
the stars are always laughing.
There are baobab trees by
the score with roots going
deep as they please without
breaking up the place
and not a single sheep
to menace my one silly rose
visible only with the heart
who speaks to me when I'm sad.
And one yellow snake
when I want to go home.

Galaxy Flight to Midnight

First they fled out of Africa,
seeking new sources of food
or maybe a change of scenery.
Then they fled the ice sheets and
dire wolves that haunted their dreams.
From hunger and drought they fled
over the Bering Strait and beyond.
From religious persecution they fled
to a New World of unbridled freedom.
From war, famine, and disease they fled
to whatever country would take them.
They fled the whips and chains
of Southern plantations to live in
crowded cities of the North,
as others fled the same cities from
immigrant hordes and dark races.
They fled into gated communities
to free themselves from people
and viewpoints not their own.
They fled into space out of boredom
and because it was the last frontier.
Finally they fled from the earth itself,
in their luxury starship cruisers,
all the way to the center of the galaxy
and a big black hole
that swallowed them up,
every last one.

The Case of the Missing Pea

Once upon a time, there
was a princess and a pea,
or so the story goes,
though in light of
recent evidence,
you might well ask
if there ever was
a real princess.
For the world is full
of would-be princesses
and princes, for that matter.

Don't you think it odd
that a woman looking like
a drenched rat suddenly
appears at the door
announcing herself as
the real McCoy?

But the Queen is not convinced.
Instead of asking for an ID,
she devises a test involving
twenty mattresses,
twenty feather beds
and a single pea, which
assumes outsized significance.

The princess aces the test,
sensing the pea
atop so many layers
she wouldn't have felt
a whale much less a pea.
Doesn't it make you wonder?
Could it be they

were in cahoots?

And what was so special
about the pea that it had to be
placed in a museum?
Supposedly it is still there,
or so the story goes,
if no one has stolen it.
What a strange way
to end a story.

Could it be there
never was a pea at all?

The Persistence of Pheromones

It came on a waft of midnight air, caressing his nostrils
with zephyr tentacles hinting of jasmine, mint, and musk
and the smell of the room after his first awakening.

It was as much a feeling as a scent, calling out to him
with thoughts not his own, as if to envelop him
in its very essence.

Vague images began to emerge that gradually
took on shapes, appearing to move organically
against a background of chaotic colors.

As he stood there, one of the shapes drew closer,
twirling and glowing so brightly above him
he could not see its true form.

And from it there came a faint hum that grew
stronger and stronger, until it seemed like a song
with three words endlessly repeated: *I am here.*

A deceptively simple declaration, yet the words evoked
so much more, loneliness and longing, but hope as well.
He ached to see more but could not.

And just as quickly as it had come, it was gone.
Alone again in the darkness, he inhaled
deeply, trying in vain to bring back the scent.

Little did he know it came on a molecule
travelling for millennia from an unknown world
through a universe of infinite possibilities.

Akin to certain pheromones observed in moths of Earth,
its purpose was to seek out and attract, but fishing from
a wider sea, unfettered by rigid questions of identity.

Each night, he would stick his head out the window,
assaulting the air with his nose,
hoping anew to recapture the scent.

Then, one night, it returned, more insistent and personal,
as if delivering a message meant only for him.
It seemed as if it were coming from somewhere deep inside him.

And with it came the same humming voice. *I am here. I am here.*
This time, there was more to the song: *Look at me. What do you
see? Worlds upon worlds of being in the otherness of all.*

As the words repeated, the smell became more intense
and he began to see a shape slowly forming above,
moving ever closer as it came into focus.

Suspended in a billowy cloud, the glowing shape shimmered
and shifted as if it could not decide whether to reveal itself,
then finally assumed its true form.

Covered in scales, it rose gently,
in a swirl of rotary transparent appendages,
hovering above him like an iridescent dust devil.

As it fluttered its large feathery antennae, one of them
brushed his face. He could see himself reflected in
each of hundreds of dark compound eyes.

The scent was overpowering. He tried to look away but could not.
There was something about the way its antennae felt against his
face that made him tingle and want to touch whatever it was.

And just as quickly as it had come, the scent and its vision
vanished. All night he sat at the window, trying to make
sense of it, and shuddered at what he had seen and felt.

But he could still see it there, swirling gently above him,
and hear its plaintive song as if calling to him. He could feel its
presence growing stronger, with an attraction he could not explain.

In the past, he had always run from such feelings.
Better to run than to face them. Better not to face the unknown
perils of a world he preferred not to examine.

All he knew was that tonight he had experienced something
beyond himself, transcending all he had ever known
or thought possible, and longed only to feel that way again.

Where Words Go to Die

Born from a womb of cerebrum and culture,
words live out their lives, then die.
They are neither baptized nor confirmed,
though a few are consecrated
in great speeches on fields of battle
and shall not perish from the earth.

Most words live modestly
just trying to be useful,
like *you* and *I, he she it* or *is*.
They don't call attention to themselves.
Maybe that's the secret to long life.

Other words flare up briefly,
igniting conversation with their
fun sounds and meanings, then burn out
leaving only ashes and chiseled names
in the graveyards of once popular media.

There was *gumfiate,* all puffed up with pride,
and *kexy,* who ended up dry and withered,
not to mention *lardlet,* the little piece
of bacon who gave so much to meat.
Great *woundikins!* Their spirits
still murmur on the wind.

You can tell when words are about to go
by who uses them. You don't hear young folks
saying *bunkum* when they mean nonsense.
It's a pity *gallivant* has grown old and feeble—
oh, the pleasures we shared on the road.

Some words grow old from overuse—
awesome, incredible, and *unbelievable*
as it sounds, and don't get me started on *unique,*
who used to be such a nice, one-of-a-kind word.

Often it's technology that shows words the door.
The world looked so bright for *floppy disk.*
Now he can't get a job anywhere,
except in government.

All words, from the moment
first uttered by their creator,
have an inalienable right
to life, however long,
and a death with dignity.
There should be some quiet place, a hospice
where words go to die.
Soft music would lightly play, as they
gaze at the garden through the window
chatting goodbyes to friends on Facebook,
making their final peace with the world.

Ways to Kill Time

There's killing time
and *killing* time,
it's all in how you
execute it.

Don't think it's dead
just because you
ignore it by
indulging in some
forgettable task,
while meanwhile
on microsecond feet
it sneaks past you
into the future,
taking with it all
that you hold dear.

You must grab it
in the here and now
and stab it with
your steely will
until it stops kicking,
though that's likely
to leave a stain.

Some prefer a less
direct approach,
perhaps one of those
secret nerve agents
impossible to
detect that will
disable its off switch
and send it into
overdrive to

die in quick
convulsions.

You could set a trap.
Think of doing
something that
makes it stand still
like that perfect day
you hoped would
last forever
or the one
that seemed to
drag on for years.
See how long
you can go
and maybe
it'll die
of boredom.

For best results,
nothing beats an
implosive device
with sufficient force—
think *really* big,
like the Big Bang
in reverse—to
send it all packing
back where it came from.

An Eye-Pleasing Assemblage

A Found Poem from Online Descriptions of Rare Books

remarkably clean and free of age spotting
no dampness or negative odors
       spine is a little shaky but still secure
somewhat stained, internally some soiling
       may have been used for purposes other than bible study

a great and eye-pleasing assemblage
       much ridiculed but lively and informative
       provocative but also outlandish
wonderfully anachronistic
a complex mystery in its own right

like a rich walled city of spires, cathedrals, palaces,
and art galleries, with winding streets
       and fragrant courtyards
full of vivid personalities

the adventures of a naked heroine
       a lush, magical world where the characters of her
imagination possess the most universal of desires

a grotesque romance
       questions our whole notion of reality
the kind of art that's poured out of a crucible

a sudden fusing of diverse materials into a rhythmic whole
       a most handsome presentation

Afterlife

If any of my 7×10^{27} citizens are listening,
here are my final instructions for the hereafter.
As you go about your new lives,
please think well of me.

All you hydrogens are to find a new future
fusing extravagantly to light up the world
in the first controlled reaction,
while you oxygens are to fill the lungs
as long as you can of that homeless woman
named Martha on life support
who used to live in the subway.
Or why not work as a team to quench
the thirst of a dying migrant in Ajo
whose name is Jesus.

Trust you carbons and nitrogens
will cook up something special,
like helping to send the first
transgender woman to Mars,
just make sure it's Mars
and not one of those pompous
outer planet gas bags.

Last but not least, you lead, cadmium and radium
folk are to seek out lying, conniving politicians
and spread to wherever you can do the most good.

About the Author

Gene Twaronite is a Tucson poet, essayist, and fiction writer. He is the author of ten books, including two juvenile fantasy novels as well as collections of essays, short stories, and poems. His first poetry book *Trash Picker on Mars* was the winner of the 2017 New Mexico-Arizona Book Award for Arizona poetry. This is Gene's third collection of poetry. Follow more of Gene's writing@www.thetwaronitezone.com.

www.ingramcontent.com/pod-product-compliance
Lightning Source LLC
Chambersburg PA
CBHW071641090426
42738CB00013B/3179